# THE HERBALIST'S HAPPY HOUR

## CRAFTED COCKTAILS & TAPAS
### from the garden

SUSAN EVANS

# DEDICATION

For my mom, whose strength and grace continue to inspire me, and my daughters, whose beauty and talent continue to amaze me, and for my husband, for his love and support.

thyme

bay

**TABLE OF CONTENTS**

# INTRODUCTION

The new craze for handcrafted cocktails has brought people out of the liquor stores and soft drink aisles and into their gardens and farmers' markets to discover the pleasures of creating their own delicious libations with fresh seasonal ingredients. Designing your own drinks and small plates is a lot less expensive, much more fun, and definitely healthier.

I'm hoping this book will motivate you to create your own flavorful foundations for drinks and dining. I promise you hours of creative fun, delectable noshing, and blissful occasions, either solo or with others.

I first started concocting garden-centered cocktails after becoming an herbalist and scrutinizing labels more closely. Have you ever looked at the ingredients on a margarita mix? Mainly chemicals, dyes, and preservatives. Why buy when you can design your own amazing, toxin-free cocktail and drink combos with easy-to-find ingredients?

Skip the pricey infused alcohol and make your own blue spruce gin and jalapeño tequila. Concoct healthy and delicious concentrates from fresh fruits, herbs, and vegetables that you can store in the fridge and use for anything from a hibiscus lime cooler to a conifer cocktail. Trade the gloppy queso, the wilted crudités with ranch dressing, and the lackluster cheese plate for tasty creations made with vibrant seasonal ingredients.

Most of the cocktail recipes in the book are also delicious in their virgin form. I have included tea and shrub recipes to be enjoyed for their health-promoting benefits and great taste.

Being an herbalist has opened up a whole new world for me. Studying and working with herbs for the last 25 years has left me continually amazed by the many ways you can use these lovely, helpful plants.

My daughters, family, and friends have undergone several unique treatments with my potions as I developed my craft and, I'm happy to say, lived to tell the tale. Using herbs and garden produce to replace store-bought items has enriched my health and self-reliance and seems to have infiltrated every part of my life. Start with your own drink recipes, and who knows what new inspirations and adventures may develop?

We in the US are often unfavorably compared with people of foreign countries for our lack of downtime, our need to constantly produce and consume. Let's cultivate the art of leisure, taking time to celebrate life, whether with a rooftop tapas party or a patio respite for one. May this book assist you in that quest.

1

# SECTION ONE
## TOOLS & TOYS

You'll need a few pieces of equipment to make your happy hour creations easy to prepare and enjoy.

**Blender** - A blender is essential for many cocktails. Pay extra and get a good one – not just for umbrella-bedecked frozen drinks, but also to perform multiple tasks.

I have a mighty VitaMix as my blender. Pricey but it pulverizes roots and berries, and makes soups, sauces, baby food, smoothies, dips, dough, and more. You can buy reconditioned ones for a discount at www.vitamix.com. You don't need a blender this powerful for cocktails, but it's nice to have.

**Wire Sieve and Cheesecloth** - For straining out herbs, fruit, and pulp.

**Peeler** - I personally prefer a horseshoe peeler, great for peeling anything from sweet potatoes to lemons.

**Microplane** - Get one with a silicone handle for easy use. You will use this for citrus zest, ginger root, lemongrass stalks, garlic and finely grated cheese among other things. They come in a variety of grating sizes.

**Funnel** - Excellent for profanity prevention in the kitchen as you try to pour the saucepan of syrup into a storage bottle.

**Citrus Squeezer** - Not essential. You can do the same thing by cutting a lemon in half and reaming it with a fork, but a citrus squeezer separates the seeds and the pulp so all you have is juice. If you are juicing an entire bag of limes for your margarita party this will come in handy.

**Glass Jars and Bottles for Storage** - I recycle all of my glass kombucha and iced tea bottles. They make great containers for storing syrups, concentrates, salad dressings, and more. I also like mason jars, but the drink bottles are easier for pouring. Consider keeping all of your food and drink ingredients in glass for nontoxic storage and better taste. You just need to get the labels off so you can put on your own and see them clearly.

---

To get the labels off, soak bottles overnight in soapy water. The next morning drain and pour boiling water into the container and let sit; this should loosen the glue so you can scrub it off. For really stubborn labels you can apply oil to the surface first and let sit for a day or two, and then follow the above procedure.

---

**Labels** - Name and date all your concoctions so you don't end up with shelves full of mystery items. You can design your own labels;

get them online or at craft stores. I frequently use masking tape and a sharpie marker for my home pantry. Easy on, easy off. For gift giving you may want to dress it up a bit.

**The Rest** - Without quality cooking tools your culinary adventures will always be a struggle. Invest in good pans, knives, and measuring cups and spoons. Thrift stores, estate sales, TJ Maxx, Marshall's, and Ross discount department stores are some of my favorite places to scout for high-quality items at good prices.

**Extraneous** - Do you view this new interest as an opportunity to go into a shopping frenzy? You'll find a wide assortment of objects available for the budding mixologist and tapas chef. An electric juicer is fun and quite versatile. It's a great machine for powering up your mornings with a veggie-filled green juice. I have a Breville compact juicer, still pretty big, which I got for under $100 on Amazon. You can find muddlers, glasses for every conceivable beverage, insulting/catchy cocktail napkins and aprons, spice grinders, decanters, fondue pots, tapas trays, appetizer plates, bowls, and so much more. Have fun building your own collection.

# SECTION TWO

# COCKTAILS, MOCKTAILS, & CONCENTRATES

## STAPLES AND WHAT TO DO WITH THEM

You will need to keep some basic ingredients on hand to provide for sudden strokes of mixology genius. You don't need to have all of these all the time. For best results, work with fresh, in-season ingredients. Your Rhubarb Rhapsody is going to taste a lot better with fresh rhubarb in April than that one you made in January with last year's rhubarb dug out of the bottom of the freezer.

Many of the recipes call for simple syrups. These will be covered in depth in Section 3.

## FRESH HERBS

Herbs are essential to the budding bartender. Buy them fresh at the grocer's or farmers' markets, or better yet, grow them yourself. Dried herbs can also be used for infusions.

Annual plants have a life cycle that lasts only one year. They grow from seed, bloom, and produce seeds in a single growing season. They need to be replanted each spring.

# GARDENING HINTS FOR GROWING YOUR OWN

Pass on the big box stores and spend a little more on plants that have been decently cared for and have an actual root ball as opposed to the oppressed millions raised on chemical fertilizers and rushed to market like overbuilt athletes on steroids. Annuals usually grow easily from seed given the right conditions. For perennials, which can require a much longer sprouting time, buy small potted plants at the nursery and garden center.

Check those tags! Because herbs are easy to grow, have few pests, and often don't require a lot of water once established, hybridized versions of them are being sold as ground covers. No one will thank you for a mouthful of woolly thyme or Russian sage.

For the best success with herb gardening, provide good drainage, especially for Mediterranean perennial herbs like thyme, sage, rosemary, and lavender. Read the directions for who likes what. More people kill off plants by overwatering than underwatering. If you are going to pot your plants in containers make sure the containers have drainage holes.

Perennials come back year after year, usually bigger and stronger if you have taken care of them.

VII

# Cocktails,
# Mocktails, &
# Concentrates

**B**ASIL - Basil is one of those annual herbs that play well with everyone. It is easy to grow and you'll find many varieties available, from the classic Genovese to citrus and Thai basil. Great for coolers, agua frescas, cocktails, and simple syrups, this is one herb that shouts summertime.

# WATERMELON BASIL
# COOLER
## (2 servings)

One of my favorite summer drinks—so refreshing!

- 2 cups cubed fresh watermelon
- ¼ cup fresh basil leaves
- 1 cup ice cubes
- 1 tablespoon fresh lime juice

**Blend in blender and enjoy!**

Want a cocktail?
Add a shot of vodka.

**C**ILANTRO - Available year-round at very reasonable prices at your grocer's, annual cilantro adds a fresh taste to all beverages. If you are a cilantro hater feel free to replace the cilantro with mint or parsley.

# CUCUMBER CILANTRO
# COOLER
## (4 servings)

Cooling and light, this is a great drink for a scorching day.

- ¼ cup fresh cilantro sprigs (you can substitute mint or parsley)

- 1 medium cucumber, peeled

- 4 oz. gin or vodka

- Juice of 2 limes

- 4 tablespoons (or to taste) lime, mint, or plain simple syrup

- Club soda or seltzer

Put all ingredients with the exception of seltzer into a blender and process until smooth. Strain through a wire strainer to remove pulp. Pour into 4 glasses, top with seltzer and ice, and serve with a cucumber slice and cilantro stalk for garnish.

# GINGER ROOT - This

spicy, readily available root is great for digestion and circulation and has a refreshing, concentrated taste. You can find fresh ginger root at most regular and ethnic grocery stores in the produce section. Peel it easily with a metal spoon and chop finely or grate to add to simple syrups and infused liquors. Goes with everything from whiskey to vodka to tea.

# GINGER/MINT TEA
## (makes 6 cups)

This tasty digestive tea can be served hot or cold.

- ¼ cup thinly sliced or grated fresh ginger root
- 6 cups water
- 1 cup fresh mint, leaves separated from stem, stems chopped

Peel ginger root by scraping with a metal spoon and cut into small slices or roughly grate. Bring water and ginger to a boil in a saucepan. Simmer on low, covered, for 20 minutes. Stir in mint leaves, turn off heat, and let steep for another 10 minutes. Strain and serve hot or cold with lemon and honey.

# HIBISCUS

**H**IBISCUS - This is the imported hibiscus flower, grown in tropic regions, not the rose of Sharon in your back yard. It has a lovely citrusy flavor and turns everything an intense ruby red. Hibiscus is a circulatory tonic and helps to lower blood pressure and cholesterol. Great in simple syrups, cocktails, and teas. You can buy it on the web, and in herb shops and Latino groceries, where it is sometimes known as Jamaica (pronounced ha-MY-ca).

# HIBISCUS
# TEA
## (1 serving)

- 1 ½ cups water
- 1 tablespoon broken-up hibiscus blossoms

Bring water to a boil and pour over hibiscus. Steep, covered, for 5-7 minutes. Strain out hibiscus, add sweetener if desired, and enjoy.

# HIBISCUS
# CHAMPAGNE
# COCKTAIL
## (1 serving)

A different take on a Kir Royale.

- 1 teaspoon hibiscus simple syrup (recipe follows)
- Champagne or prosecco

Add syrup to the bottom of a champagne flute, add champagne, and enjoy.

# HIBISCUS
# SYRUP

Great to sweeten and
flavor lemonade, limeade,
or any summer cocktail.

- 1 cup water

- 1 cup sugar

- ½ cup dried hibiscus
  flowers

Add all ingredients to a saucepan,
bring to a boil while stirring, turn
off heat, cover, and let steep for an
hour or two, strain, and refrigerate.

**L**AVENDER - Lavender is known for its skin-healing properties and soothing scent. The leaves and flower buds are great in bitters and cocktails and provide a lovely floral taste. Use sparingly—too much and your cocktail will taste like potpourri.

# LAVENDER
# LEMONADE
# FIZZ

(1 serving, easy to multiply)

Also nice without the alcohol; the kids will love it.

- Fresh juice of ½ lemon or lime
- 1 tablespoon lavender syrup (recipe follows)
- 1 oz. gin or vodka
- Seltzer or club soda

Add lemon, syrup, and alcohol of choice to glass, top with seltzer and ice, stir, and imbibe.

# LAVENDER
# SYRUP

- 2 tablespoons lavender buds, fresh or dried
- 1 cup water
- 1 cup sugar

Add all ingredients to a saucepan, bring to a boil while stirring, turn off heat, cover, and let steep for an hour or two, strain, and refrigerate.

**LEMONGRASS -** Go to your local Asian market for this one. Lemongrass adds a fresh lemony flavor to simple syrups and infused drinks. It also looks interesting cut to a reasonable length and residing in your glass as a stirrer or garnish. Peel the hard outer layers and chop, grind, or grate the inner leaves to flavor your drinks and dishes. This is another one I buy rather than grow.

**LEMON VERBENA -** This sprawling little annual has a lovely strong lemon scent and flavor. I grow it in containers in full sun. Lemon verbena is great for teas, crystallizing, infused alcohol, sugars, and syrups.

**MINT -** If you grow just one plant for your cocktail garden, this is the one I recommend. Good for digestion, mint offers that fresh, bracing flavor that works well in both alcohol and virgin drinks. From after-dinner tea to mint juleps, the many uses for mint make it an essential. Mint comes in many flavors, from peppermint to chocolate to orange.

A perennial, mint has Napoleonic tendencies. You have to either restrain it in pots or provide it with its own small empire—otherwise it will invade all surrounding territories. I threaten mine weekly with drought to keep it in line. It prefers part shade to shade, rich soil, and moist conditions.

**LEMON BALM -** This is one of my favorite perennial herbs in the mint family. Being a mint it has some domination issues. Great for those road rage nerves and that slightly off-kilter digestion, lemon balm not only helps to soothe the savage stomach and psyche, it provides a wonderful lemon mint taste in teas, syrups, and cocktails.

# GINGER/MINT
# MOJITO
## (1 serving)

This contains two tummy-soothing herbs, mint and ginger, and also makes a wonderfully refreshing mocktail.

- Fresh mint leaves to muddle (I use 1-2 stalks of mint or lemon balm)
- 1 oz. rum
- 2 tablespoons of Ginger/Mint-Infused Simple Syrup (recipe follows)
- 2 tablespoons fresh lime juice
- Seltzer or club soda

Add mint to bottom of glass, smash with a muddle or handle end of a wooden spoon, add rest of ingredients, stir, top with ice, and enjoy.

# GINGER/MINT-INFUSED
# SIMPLE
# SYRUP

- 1 thumb-sized piece of fresh ginger root
- 1 cup water
- 1 cup sugar
- 1 cup fresh mint, stalks included

Remove peel from ginger root by scraping with a metal spoon and cut into small slices. Place in a saucepan with water and sugar. Simmer on low, covered, for 20 minutes. Stir in mint leaves, turn off heat, and let steep for a few hours, strain, and bottle.

**R**OSE HIPS - One of my favorite trail snacks, rose hips are the seed pods left after the rose blooms. Sweet and somewhat citrusy, with a healthy dose of vitamin C, they add color and flavor to bitters, syrups, teas, and beverages.

# ROSE HIP/HIBISCUS
# TEA
## (makes 4-5 cups)

This is a beautiful ruby-red tea that is high in vitamin C and good for your heart. Good hot or cold.

- 2 tablespoons dried rose hips

- 2 tablespoons dried crushed hibiscus flowers

- 1 tablespoon fresh or dried orange peel

- 5 cups water

Add all ingredients to a saucepan, bring to a boil, turn down the heat, and simmer for 10 minutes. Strain, sweeten with Orange Simple Syrup if you like, and enjoy.

For a cocktail: Add ½ cup of orange juice to ½ cup of the tea, 1 tablespoon of Orange Simple Syrup, and 1 ounce of vodka.

**R**OSE WATER - You can get this lovely ingredient at Middle-Eastern grocers and upscale kitchen shops. Rose water adds a lovely floral taste to your cocktails. Jasmine and orange blossom water are other fragrant options.

# ROSY BLOSSOM
# ZINGER
## (1 serving)

- 1 cup orange juice
- 1 teaspoon Orange Simple Syrup
- 1 teaspoon rosewater or orange blossom water
- ⅛ teaspoon orange bitters
- 1 oz. vodka or gin

Blend together and serve over ice with a candied orange peel or orange slice for garnish.

**S**AGE - Another medicinal perennial, sage will add a lovely flavor to your whiskey, apple, and pear drinks. Easy to grow in a hot, sunny area, it comes in a variety of colors from purple to variegated with touches of pink and white.

# SAGE
# APPLE
# SIPPER

(1 serving)

Nice in the fall when temperatures cool. Try hot or cold.

- 1 cup apple juice or ginger beer
- 1 tablespoon organic apple cider vinegar
- 1 oz. whiskey
- 1 tablespoon Sage/Apple/ Ginger Simple Syrup

Combine and serve over ice, or heat and serve warm. Garnish with an apple slice and sage leaf.

# SAGE/APPLE/GINGER
# SIMPLE
# SYRUP

- 2 tablespoons dried sage leaf
- 1 medium Granny Smith, Jonathan, or other tart apple, cored and chopped
- ⅓ cup chopped ginger root
- 1 cup water
- 1 cup sugar

Add all ingredients to saucepan, stir while bringing to a boil, then cover and let steep for 4 hours. Strain and bottle.

**Sage is antimicrobial and helps alleviate symptoms of colds and flu. Try a tea made from a cup and a half of boiling water poured over a tablespoon of dried sage, steep for 5 -7 minutes, strain, and serve with some honey and lemon. Great for sore throats and colds. I start every winter with a big jar of dried sage for those winter nasties.**

# THYME
**THYME** - Thyme adds a robust herbal flavor to all sorts of food and libations. Lemon thyme is my favorite. Thyme is antimicrobial and is one of the ingredients in Listerine. It is very easy to grow with good drainage and full sun.

## HOT TODDY

My mother is Irish and when we got a respiratory illness she would always break out the hot toddies. It helped with the coughing, the congestion, and the whining and put us to sleep very effectively. Tastier and I have to think healthier than NyQuil. Here's my version.

- 1 cup Cinnamon/ Ginger/Thyme Tea, recipe follows
- 1 shot of your favorite whiskey
- 1 tablespoon fresh-squeezed lemon juice
- 1 tablespoon honey

Add hot tea to other ingredients and sip, wrapped in your favorite blanket, until you slip off to dreamtime.

## CINNAMON/GINGER/ THYME TEA

I always double the recipe and refrigerate the leftovers—that way refills are at hand. Drink within 4-5 days.

- 3-4 cinnamon sticks
- 2 tablespoons grated ginger
- 1½ tablespoons thyme leaves, dried or fresh
- 4 cups water

Combine all ingredients in a saucepan. Bring to a boil, cover, turn down the heat, and simmer for 15-20 minutes. Strain and feel better.

## Fruits to Use - Everything!

**B**ERRIES - Strawberries, blackberries, raspberries, blueberries. All are rich in antioxidants and flavor. Berries are a great ingredient for infused liquors, *agua frescas*, smoothies, and concentrates.

# BLUEBERRY BASIL BLAST

- 1 shot blueberry-infused vodka—see infused liquor section.

- 1 tablespoon Basil/Blueberry Simple Syrup (pg. 22)

- Juice of ½ lemon

- Seltzer

Combine vodka, simple syrup, and lemon juice, stir, add ice and seltzer, and garnish with blueberries and basil leaves speared on a toothpick.

# STONE FRUITS -

Peaches, plums, apricots, cherries. All delicious and lovely to use in syrups, infused liquors, and drinks of all varieties. Let's not forget the lovely pineapple, kiwi, pears, and apples. These fall and winter fruits are great to play with when all the peaches and melons are gone.

## CHERRY BOURBON
# BLAST

- 1 oz. bourbon
- 1 cup strong hot coffee
- 1 tablespoon Cherry/ Vanilla Simple Syrup, recipe follows

Combine and top with whipped cream and a cherry if you are feeling decadent.

## CHERRY VANILLA
# SIMPLE SYRUP

- 1 cup pitted fresh cherries
- 1 vanilla bean, seeds scraped and peel chopped. You can use 1 teaspoon of vanilla concentrate instead, added after syrup has been strained.
- 1 cup sugar
- 1 cup water

Combine all ingredients in saucepan. Bring to a boil, cover, and let sit for a few hours. Strain and bottle.

**R**HUBARB - One of my personal favorites. An easy-to-grow perennial with a short growing season that makes you appreciate it all the more. Can be used in sweet or savory drinks, compotes, syrups, bitters, and infusions. Unexpected and delicious, rhubarb pairs well with strawberries, apples, and pears. Not just for pies anymore.

# RHUBARB
# RHAPSODY
## (1 serving)

Unique and refreshing, this is one of my favorite springtime combos. The vanilla bean goes great with the tang of rhubarb.

- 1 shot vodka

- 1½ tablespoons Rhubarb/Vanilla/Orange Simple Syrup, recipe follows

- Juice of ½ fresh-squeezed lime

- Seltzer or club soda

Combine first three ingredients, top with seltzer and ice, stir, and partake.

# RHUBARB/VANILLA/ ORANGE SIMPLE
# SYRUP
(makes about 1 cup)

- 1 cup water

- 1 cup sugar

- 1 cup fresh rhubarb stalk, chopped into ½-inch pieces

- ⅓ cup fresh orange peel with white inner peel scraped off, thinly sliced

- 1 vanilla bean, seeds scraped and peel chopped (you can use 1 teaspoon of vanilla concentrate instead, added after straining)

Bring water, sugar, rhubarb, orange peel and vanilla bean (if using) to a boil. Cover, turn down heat, and simmer for 15-20 minutes. Turn off heat and let sit for a few hours. Strain through a wire strainer.

17

# MELONS AND CUCUMBERS

**MELONS AND CUCUMBERS** - Good for all manner of beverages, providing a clean, fresh taste.

**CITRUS** - Our beverages would be bereft indeed without the zing and freshness of lemons, limes, oranges, and grapefruit. From juice to garnish, citrus is essential to the well-stocked bar.

**CONIFERS** - Take a walk on the wild side when you harvest the new growth of pine, spruce, and fir. They impart a lovely forest/ citrus taste that works well in infusions, syrups, bitters, and creative garnishes. This is a taste of the unexpected. The bright green new growth will be at the very tips of the branches. Taste for flavor — they are not all the same and some taste like turpentine. You are trimming off the tips of branches; don't clip the leader, the branch that is growing out of the top of the tree.

# CONIFER VODKA
## (1 quart)

- 1 cup of new-growth needles of spruce or fir tips
- 1 quart vodka
- Quart jar

Put needles in jar, then bruise with a wooden spoon or muddle if so inclined. Pour vodka over, shake, and let sit for 2-3 weeks. Sample intermittently. Strain and enjoy that walking-in-the-woods flavor.

# CONIFER
# COCKTAIL

## (1 serving)

- 1 oz. of conifer vodka
- Freshly squeezed juice of one lime
- 1 tablespoon of Lime or Ginger Infused Simple Syrup
- Seltzer

Add vodka, simple syrup, and lime juice together in a glass, add ice and seltzer, and enjoy!

**V**EGGIES - tomatoes (really a fruit), peppers, beets, carrots, and cucumbers all add nutrition, color, and taste.

# JALAPEÑO
# TEQUILA

## (1 quart)

Wear rubber or latex gloves to make this so you can't possibly rub jalapeño juice into your eyes later.

- 4-6 jalapeños (or more if you are an insatiable heat lover), stem end removed

- 1 quart tequila

Put the gloves on; you'll thank me later. Cut peppers into crosswise slices and put into a quart jar with a plastic-coated lid.

Pour tequila over, shake, and let sit. I usually let it sit for 2 weeks but you may want to taste it every few days to make sure it agrees with your level of heat tolerance. Don't like tequila? Rum or vodka are good substitutes.

Vigorously rubbing your hands over stainless steel, such as a sink faucet, will help to remove lingering heat from hot peppers.

# SECTION THREE - INFUSIONS

Infusions are basically adding flavor ingredients to different mediums, be they alcohol, simple syrups, or other liquids. Infused ingredients add the yum to your libations.

Simple to make, they require only time. The longer you let ingredients infuse the stronger the taste. Alcohol is best when infused at least 2-3 weeks depending on ingredients.

## Simple Syrups

Simple syrups are equal parts sugar and water heated until the sugar dissolves, obliterating those pesky crystals hanging around the bottom of your glass. Not just for cocktails, simple syrups are used anywhere you would use sugar: lemonade, tea, dessert sauces, etc.

## Procedure for infused syrups:

Measurements for the following syrups are based on 1-2 cups of sugar to 1 cup of water.

For seeds and barks (cinnamon), roots (ginger), fruit peels and spices, mix the ingredients together before heating, bring to a boil, turn down heat, and cover and simmer for 15 minutes. Don't walk away—if it boils over you will have a true mess on your hands. After simmering, turn off the heat and let it sit for a few hours to infuse. For herbs and flowers bring water and sugar to a boil, add herbs and/or flowers, cover, and turn off heat. These don't need to simmer. Let them steep for a few hours.

Once the infusion is finished, strain through a metal strainer, bottle up, label, chill, and go create a new cocktail. Syrups should last about 1–2 weeks in the refrigerator. These also freeze well—just be sure to leave headspace in the container.

Some favorite combinations - Add below measurements to 1 cup of water and 1 to 2 cups of sugar and follow the directions listed above for simple syrups. You can add more of the ingredient for a stronger flavor. Always use whole leaves of herbs and whole spices, never ground. The following simple syrups work well combined with seltzer and lime or lemon juice. Add the alcohol of your choice for cocktails.

# BLACKBERRY/SAGE-

1 cup blackberries, 3 tablespoons fresh or 2 tablespoons dried sage leaves.

## BLUEBERRY/BASIL- 1 cup blueberries, ½ cup packed basil leaves and stems.

## CHERRIES/VANILLA BEAN - 1 cup pitted cherries, 1 vanilla bean with seeds scraped out, shell chopped (you can substitute 1 teaspoon vanilla extract but don't add until syrup is strained and cooled).

## GINGER SIMPLE SYRUP

- one of my favorites. Use 2-3 tablespoons of freshly grated ginger root, depending on how spicy you like it. Use a metal spoon to easily scrape off the peel before grating.

# GINGER AND LIME/ LEMON PEEL

- 2 tablespoons grated ginger peel

- 2 tablespoons sliced fresh citrus peel with the white inner pith removed.

# LAVENDER SIMPLE SYRUP

- 2 tablespoons fresh or dried lavender buds.

## LAVENDER BUDS/ VANILLA BEAN

- 2 tablespoons lavender buds

- 1 vanilla bean, seeds scraped out, shell chopped (you can substitute 1 teaspoon vanilla extract but don't add until syrup has cooled)

## LEMON PEEL OR LEMON THYME OR LEMON VERBENA

- 1 tablespoon lemon peel or lemon thyme

- 2 tablespoons fresh lemon verbena leaves.

## LEMON, LIME, OR ORANGE PEEL/ TARRAGON

- 2 tablespoons dried or fresh peel with white pith scraped off,

- 2 tablespoons fresh tarragon

## MINT/RASPBERRY

- 1 cup fresh mint sprigs

- 1 cup raspberries

## PEACH/ROSEMARY

- 1 cup chopped peach

- 1 tablespoon rosemary

## PINEAPPLE/SAGE

- 1 cup chopped pineapple

- 1 tablespoon sage leaf

# SECTION FOUR

SKIP THE LINES AND INFLATED PRICES OF THE LOCAL LIQUOR STORE AND USE FLAVORS OF HERBS, FRUITS, SPICES, VEGGIES, AND CONIFER NEEDLES TO MAKE YOUR OWN DESIGNER LIBATIONS. EASY TO DO AND YOUR CHOICES ARE LIMITLESS. GET CREATIVE AND COMBINE DIFFERENT FLAVORS.

## BASIC RECIPE

I usually infuse my alcohol in 1-quart glass canning jars with plastic-coated BPA-free lids (the standard canning lids). I put the flavoring ingredients in first and then pour the alcohol over them. Chop your fruits and veggies before they go in and muddle or mortar and pestle your herbs and spices. Shake the jar and let sit for at least 2 weeks at room temp out of direct sunlight. You can taste it every couple of days and see what you think.

# INFUSED ALCOHOL

Vodka is my favorite alcohol to infuse but you can use any variety of the hard stuff. The proportion of flavoring and bitter ingredients to alcohol depends on the ingredients. A general rule of thumb is around 1 cup of fresh ingredients including fruit or herbs and one to two tablespoons of dry ingredients, as in herbs or spices, to one quart of alcohol. Amount depends on desired taste and the flavor intensity of the ingredient. I will use less of peppercorns, lavender buds, and hot peppers than I would of cinnamon or star anise.

Always use whole spices and herbs, never ground. For preparation, split vanilla beans, slice the citrus and peppers, and muddle the fresh herbs. You can always add more ingredients if the flavor is not as intense as you would like.

Infused alcohol made with fresh produce is best stored in the fridge. This isn't necessary with dried herbs, fruits, and spices, which can be stored at room temperature.

**T**EQUILA - Tequila plays well with peppercorns, lime peel, orange peel, lemon peel, or some of each. It is also nice with dried or fresh whole chilies of all varieties, ginger root, lemongrass, and mango.

**VODKA** - Its fairly neutral taste makes vodka one of the easiest liquors to infuse. Be adventurous with herbs, fruits, spices, and veggies. Some favorites include citrus, rhubarb, berries, cherry/vanilla, lavender, hibiscus, and ginger.

**RUM** - You have your light rums and your dark rums, easily identified by their coloring. Light rums are easier to infuse but you can do both. Flavor possibilities: mango, mint, citrus, pineapple, lemongrass, hibiscus, berry, cinnamon, coconut, and cloves.

**GIN** - Gin is an already infused alcohol using vodka, juniper, and a bevy of other herbs and spices depending on the brand. You can make it more intense by flavoring it with citrus peel, juniper berry, and spices like cloves, star anise, and allspice; you can also try different fruits.

**WHISKEY** - You can get all different grades and types on this one. Flavors for infusing include sage, rosemary, pear, apple, vanilla, chocolate, cherry, and coffee.

**WINE** - Wine lends itself to subtle infusions. You can use any type of fruit and herbs such as sweet woodruff blooms, lavender, basil, thyme, elderflowers, rose petals and hips, and elderberries. Champagne and prosecco are great substitutes for seltzer and club soda. They will add a bit of intoxicating bubbly to your drinks.

# MAY WINE

This recipe goes back to pagan times, and is thought to have originated in Germany, where it is still made every spring. It was part of the maypole rituals, welcoming spring, new growth, and fertility. White wine, usually a Riesling, is infused with sweet woodruff, a lovely shade perennial that imparts a unique floral flavor. Can't find sweet woodruff? Try basil.

- Quart mason jar
- Bottle of good Riesling or other light white wine
- 1 cup fresh sweet woodruff sprigs and blooms

Muddle the sweet woodruff, add the wine, and chill. Shake it vigorously and leave for a day or two, shaking it again whenever you happen to open the fridge. Strain through a wire strainer and serve chilled with a fresh strawberry garnish and perhaps a flower or two.

# SECTION FIVE

## BITTERS

Bitters are a combination of alcohol, bitter herbs, spices, and other flavorings. They were once used as patent medicines and are making a comeback as a digestive tonic and cocktail flavoring. Bitters help with digestion by promoting enzyme production and gastric juices that work to prime the gastrointestinal system. Bitters also stimulate bile production and can help with blood sugar balance and improving and toning the digestive system. I like to take a few drops of bitters on the tip of my tongue around ten minutes before eating. Try it when you will be challenging your digestive system with a rich meal or buffet line.

Bitters will add a sassy kick to your favorite cocktails and help to balance sweetness.

# BITTERS & SHRUBS

## HOMEMADE BITTERS

Make bitters in a glass jar with a plastic-coated lid using the highest proof alcohol you can find. I use Everclear or vodka for mine. Add 2 cups alcohol to 3-4 tablespoons of dry flavoring ingredients (double the amount for fresh), and let steep for up to 4 weeks, shaking the jar whenever you think of it. Strain through a wire mesh strainer lined with cheesecloth or a coffee filter. Viola! Homemade bitters. The high-proof alcohol gives these a long shelf life.

The ingredients can be found online or at your local herb store or natural foods market.

## BITTER INGREDIENTS
### 1- 2 TABLESPOONS PER 2 CUPS ALCOHOL

- gentian - dried root or 14 drops extract
- quassia bark
- dandelion root
- burdock root
- fresh or dried orange peel
- fresh or dried lemon or lime peel
- fresh rhubarb

## HERBS AND SPICES FOR FLAVORING
### 2 TABLESPOONS PER 2 CUPS ALCOHOL

- fennel seed
- coriander seed
- juniper berry
- ginger root
- rose hips
- cardamom
- cloves
- allspice

- peppercorns
- cinnamon
- star anise
- sarsaparilla
- licorice root
- cinnamon
- mint

# ORANGE
# BITTERS

- Fresh peel from 3 oranges cut into thin slices

- 2 cups vodka

- 2 tablespoons ingredients from the herbs and spices list

Combine in a glass jar, leave on the kitchen counter or wherever you will see it, and shake a couple of times a day. After 3-4 weeks, strain and bottle. You can add honey or agave at this point if you would like to temper the bitterness. Refrigeration is not necessary.

**SHRUBS** are a drink from American colonial days made with vinegar, sugar, and fruit. They were used as a thirst quencher and refresher for workers. Shrubs are a cinch to make, plus they are good for your digestion and great for putting a bounty of seasonal produce to use. They can also add a nice tang to cocktails.

# FRUIT
# SHRUB

(makes 1 ⅓ cup concentrate)

- 1 cup berries or other fruit, washed and mashed into a bowl

- 1 cup sugar

- 1 cup organic apple cider (my favorite), champagne, or white wine vinegar

Place berries or fruit in bowl, add the sugar, and stir well. Cover and store in the refrigerator until the fruit releases its juice and starts to combine with the sugar to form a syrup, 24-48 hours.

Strain the syrup from the fruit. Press lightly on the fruit solids to release any remaining syrup.

You can use the fruit for topping ice cream or yogurt. Add the vinegar to the extracted syrup and whisk well to combine.

Pour through a funnel into a clean bottle. Cap and shake vigorously, and mark the date on the bottle. Store in the refrigerator. If sugar separates, just shake it. After a few days it should dissolve. Dilute the shrub with about 3 parts water or seltzer to 1 part shrub. Serve over ice.

These can also be added straight to cocktails as a flavoring agent. Shrubs last 3 weeks in the refrigerator.

# PLUM/LAVENDER
# SHRUB

- 1 cup cored and diced plums

- 2 teaspoons lavender flowers

- 1 cup sugar

- 1 cup organic apple cider vinegar

Mix plums, lavender, and sugar together and stir well. Cover and refrigerate for 24-48 hours. Strain out the syrup from the solids, add the vinegar, pour into a mason jar or glass container with a nonmetal-lined lid, and shake well.

Keep in the refrigerator for 3-4 days, shaking the jar a few times a day. Once ready dilute with 3 parts water or seltzer to 1 part shrub. So refreshing!

**GET CREATIVE AND EMBELLISH THAT DELICIOUS COCKTAIL WITH AN EYE-CATCHING GARNISH.**

33

SECTION SIX

# DRINK
## GARNISHES

Consider growing some edible flowers for garnishing. Edible flowers are not only beautiful in the garden, they also make a lovely addition to your cocktails, salads, tapas, and desserts. Use them to add that wow factor. Adorn your dishes just before serving—don't subject the flowers to heat or they will wilt. Some of my favorites include any herb flower such as cilantro, chives, basil, or dill.

Other lovely garnishes include pansies, nasturtiums, lilacs, arugula, sunflower petals, daylilies, dandelions, and hollyhocks. Pick flower buds before they have fully bloomed. For large flower heads like pansies or dandelions (yes, dandelions), pull out the individual petals or slice into colorful strips. Try a tiny bit if this is your first time eating this flower and then you can increase portions once you know you will not have a reaction. Do make absolutely sure your flower is edible and that you have identified it correctly; some flowers are truly deadly.

# CANDIED EDIBLE FLOWERS AND HERB LEAVES

Add an artfully arranged candied flower to your drinks to really wow your guests. Paper umbrellas just can't compete. These also look lovely on cupcakes, puddings, and fruit salads and will dress up any kind of dessert. Candy them in the summer and bring them out all winter long to secure your title as chef extraordinaire.

## YOU WILL NEED:

- 1 organic egg white, lightly whipped, or Just Whites, a powdered mix you can get in the baking section that you mix with water until you have achieved the desired consistency.

- Superfine granulated sugar—you can buy this or make your own by putting regular sugar in a blender or food processor until it reaches superfine texture. You will end up with powdered sugar if you let it go too long.

- Thin artist's paintbrush like the ones in cheap watercolor kits at the dollar store.

- A baking tray lined with parchment or wax paper.

- Flowers or leaves of choice –my personal favorites include fuchsias, lemon balm, chocolate mint, mint, pansies and violets, rose petals, and lavender sprigs. Just make sure you have a truly edible ingredient that has not been sprayed with pesticides.

Candy your flowers as soon as possible after picking, otherwise they will wilt. I pick a few flower or mint stalks, put them immediately in a glass with some water to keep them from wilting, pull off the flowers or leaves as I process them, then go pick some more.

To candy, dip the paintbrush in your egg white and carefully paint all surfaces of the leaf or flower. Gently sprinkle sugar on the flower, covering all surfaces. Shake off excess sugar. Place flower face up on the parchment paper and allow to dry until stiff. Store in a tightly covered container between sheets of parchment paper.

# CANDIED

## CITRUS PEELS

Great for drink and pastry garnishes. You can make these with oranges, lemons, or limes. Organic fruit is the best, but if you are not using organic, scrub the outside of the fruit with warm soapy water, rinse well, and let dry.

- Peel from 4-5 oranges or 6-8 limes or lemons with inner white pith scraped off
- 1 ½ cups sugar

Cut the fruit into quarters and carefully separate the peel from the fruit. Use the fruit for another recipe or juice for drinks. Scrape the peel with a metal spoon (grapefruit spoons are great for this) to get off as much of the white pith as possible. Slice scraped peel into strips, cover with water in a saucepan, and bring to a boil. Turn the heat down and simmer for 5 minutes. Strain out the water.

Add 1 cup of the sugar to 1 cup water, bring to a boil, reduce heat, and add drained peels. Simmer for about ½ hour until tender. Strain off the orange simple syrup with a metal strainer and use for sweetening drinks and cocktails. Separate the peels on a wire rack to cool.

Take remaining ½ cup sugar and blend in a mixer or food processor until it is superfine (but don't go too long or you will get powdered sugar). Roll peels in superfine sugar and place on wire rack to dry. Once dry, store in airtight container. You can also dip in chocolate once they are dried.

# SALTS AND SUGAR

## RIMMERS

I have friends who pay ridiculous prices for flavored salts and sugars. Make your own creative combos with spices and herbs.

## LEMON, LIME, AND ORANGE RIMMERS

Pulverize dried citrus peel of choice in blender and add it to an equal amount of salt or sugar. Combine and store in a covered glass container.

## CHILE FLAVORED

Use 1 teaspoon chili powder of choice (I like chipotle), add to ½ cup salt or sugar.

# HERB AND SPICES

Add 1 teaspoon dried herb or spice of choice to ½ cup salt or sugar.

You can also use cocoa powder, smashed peppermint candies—anything edible you can pulverize that will stick to a glass.

To use: Pour flavored salt or sugar onto a plate, moisten the rim of your glass with a lime or lemon slice, dip the glass into the salt/sugar, and viola! Instant panache. Use flavored salts and sugars to add unique tastes to all your dishes.

# HERB AND FLOWER ICE CUBES

For an elegant touch try these.

Fill ice cube trays halfway with water, freeze. Take out trays, position your fresh herbs or edible flowers on top of the ice cubes, and add more water. Reposition if necessary and freeze. Lovely!

# SECTION SEVEN
# TAPAS
# AND TASTY
# BITES

What is a cocktail party without tasty nibbles? I like to keep my snacks simple and easy to prepare beforehand, and to eat them with my fingers or the aid of a toothpick. Can we just once and for all skip the chopped aged vegetables with bottled ranch dressing and the bottled salsa with tortilla chips? Come on, people! We can do better than that.

# PROSCIUTTO-WRAPPED
# PLUMS & PEACHES

A delicious celebration of summer fruits that makes an impressive presentation.

- Ripe plums or peaches, halved, pits removed, cut into a little larger than bite-size wedges

- Gorgonzola, goat, or blue cheese

- Milk, enough to make cheese spreadable

- Prosciutto slices

- Balsamic reduction (recipe follows)

- Thyme and chopped chives for garnish

Preheat oven to 350°. Add a small amount of milk or cream to cheese of choice and mash until creamy enough to spoon onto the fruit wedges.

After adding the cheese, wrap the wedge with prosciutto. Roast in the oven for about 8-10 minutes on a greased baking sheet until heated through. Serve warm, drizzled with balsamic reduction and topped with fresh thyme and chopped chives.

For the streamlined no-bake version you can cut the fruit into quarters (cheese is optional), wrap with prosciutto, and serve. It is still quite tasty if not as impressive

# BALSAMIC
## VINEGAR REDUCTION

Add 2 cups of balsamic vinegar to a saucepan. Bring to a boil, then turn down heat to a simmer until it is thickened and reduced to ½ - 1 cup, depending on how thick you want it. This will concentrate the flavor. Cool, bottle in glass, and store in the fridge. Usually takes about 15-20 minutes.

# DATE AND GOAT CHEESE-STUFFED PEPPADEWS IN PROSCIUTTO WITH WINE REDUCTION

(makes 20)

My winter version of the above recipe. You can find peppadew peppers in the deli section of most supermarkets in the olive bar. Turn them over on paper towels to drain before stuffing. You could also use fresh mini sweet peppers.

- 1 5-6 oz. tube soft goat cheese – can also use bleu or gorgonzola cheese
- Milk, just enough to make cheese spreadable if necessary
- ¼ cup dried currants, apricots, or dates, chopped
- 20 peppadew peppers
- 2 3 oz. packages of prosciutto
- Dash of cocoa
- Dash of paprika
- Marsala Wine Reduction (recipe follows)

Drain the peppers by placing upside down on paper towels. Mix the goat cheese and chopped fruit, add some milk or cream as necessary. Fill drained peppadews with cheese mixture; I use the handle end of a regular spoon to insert the cheese in the pepper.

Wrap with a strip of the prosciutto and arrange on a baking tray.

Bake at 350 for 8-10 minutes until heated through, drizzle with wine reduction and serve.

# MARSALA
## WINE REDUCTION

- 2 cups Marsala or other red wine

- ½ teaspoon cocoa powder

- 1 teaspoon smoked paprika or other ground pepper of choice

- Add cocoa and paprika to 2 cups of Marsala or other red wine; reduce to ½ cup over low heat.

# ANTIPASTO
## PLATTER

A favorite easy appetizer with definite appeal is an antipasto platter. Procure an assortment of cheese, sausages, and roasted veggies. You can get all of these ready-made at the local deli. Add some paté, fig or quince jam, a stem or two of purple grapes, and strawberries, add an assortment of crackers, and call it done. An easy standby when you don't have time to cook. Cut the cheeses into cubes or slices, roll the ham and cut sausage into bite-size pieces, cut the roasted veggies so they are ready for plucking, and put out the toothpicks.

Arrange it artfully on a platter and embellish with a few herb sprigs or edible flowers. Put the crackers on a separate plate for easy access and put out bowls of olives and unique pastes, jams, or mustards with serving knives and spoons. Easy and delicious.

# GARLIC SHRIMP
# GAMBOS A AJILLO

A classic Spanish tapa, shrimp with garlic is delicious and a snap to make. Don't overcook the shrimp; they will go from tender and succulent to hard and rubbery.

- 1 lb. medium shrimp, peeled and deveined, nice with tails left on

- 1 tablespoon oil

- 2 tablespoons butter

- 6-8 medium garlic cloves sliced thin, or better yet, 10-12 whole cloves of roasted garlic (you can find these at deli olive bars or roast your own)

- 1 teaspoon chives, chopped

- 1 tablespoon parsley, chopped

- 1 teaspoon chili pepper flakes (optional)

Melt butter with oil in a skillet over low heat. Add raw garlic if using and sauté until golden. If you are using the roasted garlic add the shrimp and garlic together and stir, cooking over medium heat, turning once until opaque, about 2 minutes per side. Top with chives and parsley. Serve warm with sliced baguette.

# HERB PESTO
# CHEESE
# TORTA

This is truly impressive and deceptively easy.

- 1 cup pesto (recipe follows)
- 1 cup feta cheese, cut into small cubes
- 1 cup sun-dried tomatoes in oil, drained and sliced

Spray a small shallow glass container with cooking oil. Cut an oversized piece of plastic wrap to line the container and overlap the edges. Push the plastic wrap in and spread it out evenly to line the sides and bottom of the container, and make sure there is an overlap on all sides.

Put down a layer of sundried tomatoes, followed by feta cheese, followed by pesto. Press down firmly with the back of a spoon after each layer. Make sure you can see each layer when looking at the side of the container. You can do thick layers and be done, or do thinner layers and repeat the process. Chill for at least 8 hours.

Lift the torta out of the container by turning the container over onto a serving plate, gently pulling down on the plastic wrap if necessary as it releases onto the plate. Peel off the plastic wrap, top with a basil leaf or some edible flowers, surround with crackers, and admire your masterpiece.

You can also add chopped green or black olives as one of the layers.

# PESTO

I love pesto; you can use it for so many things and change up ingredients for different taste profiles. Pesto is usually made with basil but you can make pesto with any leafy herb from the garden or market. I make sage/walnut pesto for pork, mint/cashew for lamb, and cilantro/peanut pesto for Thai and Mexican food. Just substitute different nuts and herbs.

- ¼ cup toasted pine nuts or walnuts

- ⅓ cup olive oil (add more if needed—you want a thick sauce texture)

- 1 cup fresh basil

- ½ cup shredded Parmesan cheese

- 2-3 cloves of fresh garlic

Add all ingredients to a food processor or blender and process until smooth, adding more oil if necessary. Use on pastas, sandwiches, roasted vegetables, potatoes, and more.

Toasting shelled nuts gives them a rich, roasted flavor. Preheat oven to 350. Spread the raw nuts, using only one variety at a time, evenly on a baking sheet. Roast regular nuts like walnuts, pecans, and cashews for around 6-10 minutes, depending on the size of the nut. Pine nuts I do on the stove so I can keep an eye on them. Put them in a dry skillet over medium heat. I prefer cast iron for this but use whatever you have. Shake them gently until they turn golden and remove immediately to a cool plate. Easiest? Just buy them roasted.

# SUN-DRIED TOMATO AND CANNELLINI
## DIP WITH PITA CHIPS

Another easy dish made with ingredients available year-round.

- 1 15 oz. can cannellini or other white beans, drained and rinsed
- 1 cup sun-dried tomatoes in oil, roughly chopped
- 1 clove garlic, minced
- 1 tsp fresh or dried rosemary
- 2 tablespoons olive oil
- 2 tablespoons lemon juice
- 2 tablespoons pitted Kalamata olives
- Salt and pepper to taste
- Dash of chili pepper (optional)
- Water * to add if too thick
- Pita chips

Put all ingredients other than pita chips and olives into a food processor.

Puree and serve, topped with chopped olives and a side of pita or tortilla chips.

47

# MARINATED
# CITRUS-
# HERB
# OLIVES AND
# ARTICHOKES

(makes about 3 cups)

This needs to sit for a while for the best flavor so make it a day or two ahead of when you will need it. Remember to bring it to room temperature before serving or you will have olive oil glop instead of marinade.

- 2 cups mixed olives of your choice
- 1 15 oz. jar of quartered artichoke hearts, drained
- 1 teaspoon dried or fresh thyme leaves
- 1 teaspoon dried or fresh rosemary
- 2 tablespoons lemon juice
- Grated zest of 1 lemon
- 3-4 cloves garlic, minced
- 1/4 cup extra-virgin olive oil
- Freshly ground pepper, to taste
- 1 teaspoon of red pepper flakes (optional)

Drain olives and artichokes on paper towels. Combine all ingredients in a medium bowl and mix well. Cover and refrigerate for 1-2 days, stirring several times.

# SPICED NUTS

(makes 2 cups)

I love this recipe and have to stop myself from eating the whole batch once they are done. Use cashews, walnuts, pecans— whatever you like, or do a mix. Great for gifts.

- 2 cups raw nuts, about 10 ounces, whatever kind you like

- ½ cup brown sugar

- 1 teaspoon salt

- 1 teaspoon cayenne pepper, more if you like it hot

- 1 teaspoon paprika

- 1 teaspoon cinnamon

- 1 teaspoon coriander

- 1 teaspoon cumin

- ½ teaspoon black pepper

- 1 organic egg white, lightly whipped

Preheat the oven to 325°. In a small bowl, mix the sugar with the salt and spices. In a different bowl whisk the egg white until frothy. Add the nuts and spiced sugar mix to the egg white and stir until the nuts are all well coated. Spread out the nuts in an even layer on a baking tray lined with Silpat or parchment paper and bake for about 25-30 minutes until browned, stirring once halfway through and breaking up the nuts. Move them from the baking tray onto a plate or tray to stop further browning. Cool and enjoy.

# SMOKED
# SALMON
# MOUSSE

## (makes about 1½ cups)

This is so easy and tasty it's criminal. I usually serve it with a side of capers and finely diced red onion, but you can serve as is and it will be a hit.

- 1 cup smoked salmon

- ½ cup cream cheese, softened

- ¼ cup softened butter

- Capers and chopped red onion for garnish

Blend the butter, salmon, and cream cheese in a food processor. Place in a bowl and garnish with capers and finely chopped red onion. Serve with crackers or crostini. Simple and superb. Recipe can be doubled.

# SICILIAN
# BRUSCHETTA

This is a fresh, easy topping that you can also use on baked chicken, fish, or pizza. You can also add a sliced avocado and have it as a side salad.

- 1 cup farm-fresh tomatoes or cherry tomatoes diced fine
- 2 tablespoons finely chopped green onion
- 2 tablespoons roasted red peppers, chopped
- 1-2 tablespoons fresh basil, chopped
- Fresh basil leaves for garnish
- 1-2 cloves garlic, minced (about 1 teaspoon)
- 3 tablespoons chopped pitted olives
- 1-2 teaspoons capers, rinsed and chopped
- 2 teaspoons extra virgin olive oil, plus more for brushing toasts
- 1 teaspoon balsamic vinegar
- Dash of red pepper flakes
- Salt and pepper to taste
- Goat cheese or slices of Manchego cheese
- Crusty bread, sliced fairly thin, brushed with olive oil and lightly toasted or grilled.

Mix all ingredients except for bread in a small bowl and set aside for about an hour. If holding longer than an hour, keep in refrigerator but return to room temperature to serve.

Spoon onto toasted, oiled bread slices and serve. Top with goat cheese, Manchego, or fresh baby mozzarella and add a basil leaf for garnish.

# FRUIT, GOAT CHEESE, AND PISTACHIO
# TRUFFLES
## (makes 20)

This is a super-easy little bite that you can make ahead of time. I usually have all these ingredients on hand so it's a great recipe for potlucks and last-minute guests when you're not sure you have enough food.

- 1 ½ cups of shelled pistachios (can also use cashews or mixed nuts)

- 1 8 oz. log of goat cheese at room temperature

- 1 cup of dried fruit— apricots, cranberries, whatever you like— diced into small pieces (you can also use whole grapes instead of the dried fruit)

Chop pistachio nuts in a food processor. Don't process too long or you will have pistachio butter. Mix together the goat cheese and dried fruit. Roll into 20 small balls. Lightly roll the balls in the ground pistachios to coat. Chill ½ hour before serving.

*For grapes: Cover a washed, dried grape with the goat cheese and roll in the nuts.*

# BABY CRAB CAKES WITH SRIRACHA/ CHIVE AIOLI

(makes 12 mini crab cakes or 4 full-size cakes)

This is an elegant dish. As I explain below you can brown these in a pan or bake them. After discovering the baking option it's my pick for a crowd as it is a lot easier and the cakes are less likely to fall apart. I like to take fresh chive leaves and cut them to make a star on top of the cakes with a chive blossom or other edible flower in the center.

- 2 tablespoons mayonnaise
- 1 tablespoon fresh lemon juice
- 1 teaspoon Dijon mustard
- 1 egg, beaten
- 2 cups cooked lump crabmeat, cleaned of all shells
- few drops of Tabasco, to your taste
- 2-3 chopped scallions
- ¾ cup bread crumbs, ¼ for mixing, ½ for coating; Panko crumbs work great
- Butter and/or olive oil

Combine ingredients gently in a bowl, reserving ½ cup of the bread crumbs. Shape into small individual rounds, press into a patty shape and lightly coat each side with bread crumbs. Chill, covered, in the refrigerator for an hour.

To pan fry, coat the inside of a skillet with half butter and half oil, enough to cover. Cook the cakes on each side until they are a golden brown, carefully turning once. An alternative method is to place the crab cakes on a greased baking sheet and bake in a pre-heated 375° oven for 15 minutes. They don't brown as nicely but are still quite tasty, and this is easier if you'll be serving a crowd.

Put on a torn butter lettuce sleeve and serve with a dollop of sriracha/chive aioli and chopped chives.

53

# SRIRACHA/CHIVE AIOLI

- 1 cup good mayonnaise, not low-fat
- 1-2 teaspoons chopped chives; chive flowers are a nice alternative
- 1 teaspoon sriracha or chili sauce, more or less depending on taste
- 1 tablespoon fresh-squeezed lemon or lime juice

Combine ingredients and serve with crab cakes.

# CREAM CHEESE AND OLIVE DIP

An Evans classic, easy and surprisingly addictive. While my family members try to come up with competitively superior appetizers for our annual appetizer parties, someone invariably shows up with this lazy offering and it is the first thing eaten and the first empty bowl. Deliciousness is not always labor intensive.

- 1 package cream cheese, room temp
- 1 cup drained pimiento-stuffed olives
- Milk if needed to loosen it into dip consistency

For a rustic version you can chop the olives and mash them into the softened cream cheese. For a smoother version, put ingredients in a food processor and pulse until blended. Add milk little by little if it's too stiff to dip. Serve with your favorite potato chips and call it done.

# MARINATED FLANK STEAK WITH ROASTED PEPPERS AND CHIMICHURRI SAUCE

This is an easy do-ahead appetizer that can be served warm or cold. This is also a delicious summer salad, great sliced and served on greens with cherry tomatoes and other summer veggies with some bleu cheese dressing.

## MARINADE

- ⅓ cup olive oil
- ¼ cup soy sauce
- 1 tablespoon Worchester sauce
- 1 tablespoon sambal oelek or sriracha sauce
- 3 cloves minced garlic
- 1 teaspoon honey or agave
- Fresh cracked pepper
- 1 ½ lbs. flank steak

Whisk first seven ingredients together and place in a baggie or shallow dish. Add steak, cover, and marinate overnight. Cook steak over medium heat on the grill, about 4 minutes per side, let rest and then slice against the grain, cutting into slices you can fold onto a toothpick.

## CHIMICHURRI SAUCE

Use on all types of grilled and roasted meats, fish, and veggies.

- 1 cup fresh Italian parsley
- ⅓ cup balsamic vinegar
- ½ cup olive oil
- 2 garlic cloves, minced
- ¾ tsp red pepper flakes
- 1 teaspoon oregano
- ½ teaspoon cumin
- ½ teaspoon salt

Combine in food processor.

### TO ASSEMBLE:

- Flank steak pieces
- Roasted red peppers cut into bite-size pieces
- Chimichurri sauce

Using toothpicks, spear a pepper slice, add on a steak slice, and serve the chimichurri sauce on the side for dipping.

# PINEAPPLE/ SAUSAGE
## SKEWERS

- Kielbasa, chorizo, or other cooked sausage link of choice, cut into one-inch slices

- Fresh pineapple chunks, roughly the same size as the sausage

In a heated skillet add just enough oil to coat the bottom of the pan. Add sausage slices and cook over medium heat until they have browned on one side; turn over with a fork and brown the other side. Let cool enough to handle and arrange a fresh pineapple chunk with a sausage slice on a toothpick. Repeat. Nice served with spicy mustard.

You can also caramelize the pineapple by cooking it as you did the sausage; its appearance will be better if you do it in a separate batch, perhaps in the same skillet but ahead of the sausage.

# OTHER IDEAS FOR TAPAS

- Steamed edamame with smoked sea salt

Anything on a skewer—toothpicks are perfect:

- Cherry tomatoes cored and stuffed with pesto

- Cherry or grape tomatoes wrapped in a basil leaf with a boccorini (baby mozzarella ball )and speared on a toothpick

- Prosciutto-wrapped melon, shrimp, or cheese chunks. Really, prosciutto-wrapped anything

- Crostini or crackers topped with:

  - Manchego cheese and sliced chorizo sausage

  - Avocado slices, shrimp, and sriracha/chive aioli

- Butter and thin slices of baby radish and sea salt

- Manchego cheese, sun-dried tomatoes, and roasted garlic cloves

- Baked small rounds of sweet potato or butternut squash topped with pesto

- Goat cheese blended with thyme or rosemary and topped with fruit chutney

# INDEX

## BIO

Susan Evans is an herbalist who lives in the foothills of Colorado. After managing garden centers and greenhouses on the front range she operated her own landscaping company installing gardens for commercial and residential clients. Changing focus she attended The Rocky Mountain Center for Botanical Studies, receiving certification through their advanced program in clinical herbalism. She now owns Chrysalis Herbs where she teaches extensively on herbs and their many uses in cooking, healing, gardening and crafting along with classes on wild foraging. You can find her at www.chrysalisherbs.com.

Made in the USA
San Bernardino, CA
17 December 2019

61771083R00046